Preface

I wrote this book with one purpose. It is to promote "kindness" among mankind.

We all live in this one beautiful earth. We are interdependent on each other for the world to function properly. Hence, we are just one big human family! Kindness is the beginning of all goodness; respect, responsibility, love, happiness, etc.

So let's be kind and make our big family a happy one!

About the Author

I am a stay-at-home mother of two, an eleven-year old daughter and an eight-year old son. They are my heart and soul. I have brought them up to be good and kind persons. And they are. To me, they are the best kids!

As a parent, I want to see them grow up to be responsible adults and be happy. However, the world we live in has gone astray and is going in the wrong direction. It is being filled with unpleasant things; division, hatred, racism, wars, famine, greed, etc. It has saddened me. I want to fix it for my children, like any parent. But I am just a little voice, a tiny ant in this giant world. What can I do?

So I wrote this book. It is for children because the future depends on them. My wish is to spread the idea about being kind in order to make this world a better place. I wish my book would make parents and children start thinking and talking about accepting others, whoever they are, and taking care of family, friends and neighbors by helping and sharing. This is my first small step to try to make a difference. We can start from one family, one school, one community, one town and so on.

We are all little ants walking around in this giant world, doing this and that. But are we doing anything meaningful? Are we doing things that help make the world a better place? Let's be kind and do good deeds. The goal is for us and the next generations to live happily and enjoy life at its best.

Let's do this together!

"Ant Ville"

Happy Time
In Ant Ville

Part 1

Mom Ant: Good morning, Sunshines!

Andrew Ant: Good morning!

Mom Ant: Did you have a good-night sleep?

Andrew and Annie Ants: Yes, we did.

Dad Ant: Good morning, kiddos! Are you ready for breakfast?

Annie Ant: Yes, I am. What is for breakfast, Dad?

Dad Ant: We are having pancakes and honey. How does that sound?

Annie Ant: It sounds great!

Andrew Ant: Yum!

Dad Ant: Here we go. Eat up! You both are growing and need a good breakfast.

Andrew and Annie Ants: Thanks, Dad!

Mom Ant: What is the plan for today, kids?

Andrew Ant: We are going to play soccer at the field with our friends.

Annie Ant: And I want to go on the swing after that. I love the swing!

Dad Ant: Well..have fun and play nice!

Andrew and Annie Ants: We will.

Andrew Ant: Hi Alex! Are you ready to go play?

Alex Ant: Hi guys! Yes, I am. Let's go!

Arron Ant: Hey guys, wait for me! ... Bye Mom!

Arron's Mom: Have fun, Son! Thanks again for your help cleaning up!

Arron Ant: No problem, Mom!

Annie Ant: Arron, how nice! Did you really help your Mom?

Arron Ant: Yes, I did. And it makes her happy.

Andrew Ant: Are we all here, guys?

Atom Ant: Yes, I think so. There should be eight of us.

Amber Ant: Yes, there are eight.

Arron Ant: Should we play on the same teams as last time, guys?

Annie Ant: Yes, I am fine with that.

Arthur Ant: Me too.

Arron Ant: Angie, do you want to kick the ball to start?

Angie Ant: Sure. Let's play!

Andrew Ant: Mom...Dad..wait up! Where are you going?

Dad Ant: Hey kids! We are going to the farm to get some corn and honey.

Mom Ant: We are running out of them. Are you done playing?

Annie Ant: Yes, we are.

Dad Ant: How was the soccer game?

Andrew Ant: It was fun!

Annie Ant: Can we come with you to the farm?

Dad Ant: Of course!

Andrew Ant: I can help pick the corn.

Annie Ant: Me too.

Dad Ant: That is wonderful! How sweet of you both to offer!

Andrew Ant: We are bigger now. We can help.

Annie Ant: Arron helped his Mom clean up after breakfast. I think we are ready to help you with some chores, too.

Mom Ant: Aww...that makes me super happy!

Dad Ant: Thanks, kiddos!

Mom Ant: Dinner is ready!

Andrew Ant: Ooh...cantaloupe! My favorite!

Annie Ant: It looks so good!

Dad Ant: It is fresh, right off the vine.

Mom Ant: And this is the honey we got from the farm today.

Andrew Ant: We are so lucky with all this yummy food.

Annie Ant: Yes, we are.

Mom Ant: Well, let's eat.

Andrew Ant: We are ready to help you clean up, Mom.

Annie Ant: Yes, how do we do it?

Mom Ant: Here are damp cloths. Wipe the leaves gently so you do not tear them. Then put them back on the shelf.

Dad Ant: Your Mom and I will be over here peeling off some corn husks.

Andrew Ant: This is fun!

Annie Ant: And easy.

Mom Ant: Great job, sweeties! Thank you!

Mom Ant: Did you both wash your hands and brush your teeth?

Andrew and Annie Ants: Yes, we did.

Mom Ant: Very good!

Dad Ant: What are we reading tonight?

Andrew Ant: I picked my favorite book about airplanes.

Annie Ant: I wish I could fly like a plane. It would be so much fun!

Mom Ant: Yes, it would be.

Dad Ant: How about you take turns reading one page at a time?

Mom Ant: And remember to turn off the lights when you finish.

Andrew Ant: I will, Mom.

Mom Ant: Good night, kids! Sweet dreams!

Dad Ant: Good night! Don't let the bed bugs bite!

Andrew and Annie Ants: Haha... You're funny, Dad. Good night!

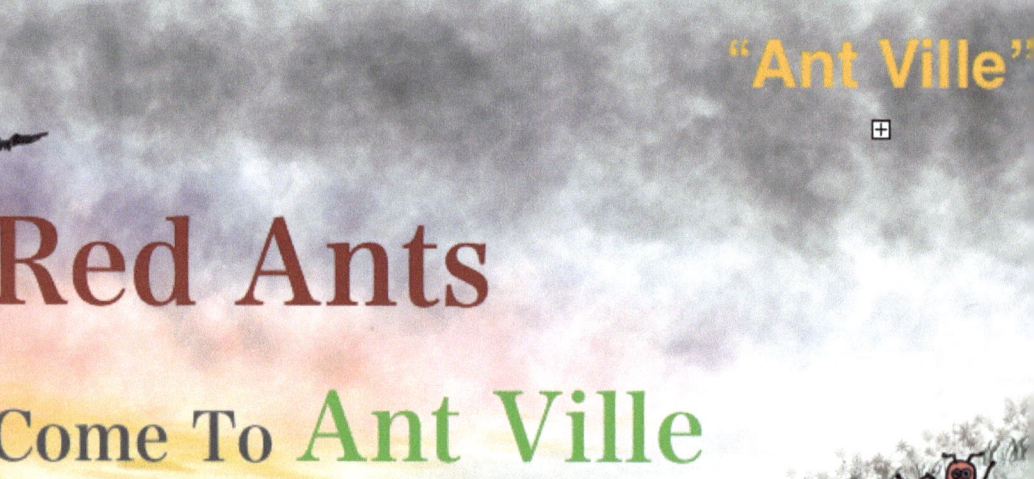

Red Ants

Come To Ant Ville

"Ant Ville"

Part 2

Andrew Ant: Mom, can I have pancakes for breakfast today?

Annie Ant: We haven't had them for over a week.

Mom Ant: I am sorry, kids! We still can not have any pancakes.

Dad Ant: We are having some corn.

Andrew Ant: The corn is not fresh any more, Dad. It is dry!

Mom Ant: I know, honey. But that is all we have for now.

Annie Ant: Why, Mom?

Mom Ant: That is because we are not allowed to go to the farm.

Dad Ant: The Red Ants have moved in and they do not want to share the farm with anyone.

Andrew Ant: That is not nice!

Annie Ant: Why do they do that?

Dad Ant: Well..we don't know.

Mom Ant: They know that we all live on the food from there. But they don't seem to care.

Annie Ant: That makes me sad!

Red Ant Dad: Hey, kids! You can not play here. Our family wants the field all to ourselves.

Annie Ant: Why?

Andrew Ant: It is a big field. There is enough room for everybody.

Alex Ant: And we can take turns on the swing.

Red Ant Mom: No, we do not want to share!

Annie Ant: I don't understand!

Andrew Ant: Let's go home. I don't want to play here any more.

Red Ant Dad: This is our field now. We will not let anybody play here. We can do whatever we want.

Red Ant Son 1: Yay!

Red Ant Son 2: Yippie...I don't like to wait and take turns on the swing.

Red Ant Daughter 1: Me neither.

Red Ant Mom: The other ants can go find some other field to play at.

Red Ant Dad: That's right. Let's take the soccer ball home too.

Red Ant Dad: Hey kids, why are you playing together? We red ants only play with red ants.

Red Ant Mom: You should go home and only play with your brother or sister ants.

Andrew Ant: But we always play and have fun together.

Annie Ant: And we are best friends!

Red Ant Dad: We think it is a bad idea.

Red Ant Mom: Yes, it is a bad idea!

Andrew Ant: The Red Ants make everybody mad and sad, Dad.

Dad Ant: I know. Since they moved in, there is only trouble.

Mom Ant: They take all the food.

Annie Ant: They have taken over our playground.

Andrew Ant: I can't play with my friends any more.

Mom Ant: There should be something we can do about this.

Dad Ant: I agree. We need to fix it.

Annie Ant: Angie, what are you doing?

Angie Ant: Arron took the bread basket that I found.

Arron Ant: But it is mine! I left it there when I went looking for my kite.

Arron's Mom: Angie, that is our basket, honey.

Angie Ant: Oh no! I'm sorry! I was so happy to find bread. We are running out of food at our house. Here Arron...you can have it back.

Andrew Ant: This is awful! We can not go out. Our friends are not coming outside because the Red Ants scared them. And we are running out of food.

Annie Ant: I miss my friends. I miss playing with them.

Andrew Ant: Me too.

Annie Ant: I do not like this at all!

Andrew Ant: We have to do something.

Annie Ant: What can we do?

Andrew Ant: I don't know yet.

Andrew Ant: What do we have left for dinner, Mom?

Mom Ant: We have some old bread tonight.

Annie Ant: Is that it?

Dad Ant: Unfortunately, yes.

Andrew Ant: What are we going to do tomorrow?

Mom Ant: We will figure something out, kids. We have to.

Dad Ant: I will go check the beehive. I will take the long way so the Red Ants will not see me and block me again.

Mom Ant: It's time for bed, kids.

Andrew Ant: Okay, Mom.

Annie Ant: I might have nightmares about the Red Ants again tonight, Mom.

Mom Ant: Let us say a prayer for you to have a nice dream, and for the bad things to go away. Okay?

Annie Ant: Okay.

Dad Ant: We will keep the faith and trust that good things will happen to us, good ants.

"Ant Ville"

Happiness Returns
To Ant Ville

Part 3

Leader Ant: Welcome to our emergency meeting, fellow ants! We have a lot to discuss today.

Dad Ant: The main worry for us is that we are running out of food.

Green Ant Dad: I have a big empty field. Everyone is welcome to come and plant food.

Leader Ant: That is a wonderful idea!

All Dad and Mom Ants: We are in!

Leader Ant: I have a lot of seeds for us to start with. If we work together, we can have the new farm ready in no time!

Green Ant Dad: We finished raking and pruning the soil yesterday. Today we can plant the seeds.

Purple Ant Dad: We have cantaloupe seeds and we will use the first row.

Yellow Ant Dad: We have corn seeds and we will use this third row.

Dad Ant: We have pumpkin seeds here.

Blue Ant Mom: This is great. We should get our first crops very soon.

Dad Bee: Hi, my ant friends! We have not seen you for a while, so we brought you some honey.

Mom Bee: We know how much you and your kids love it.

Dad Ant: You are kind and generous, my bee friends! Thank you for flying all the way to deliver it to us.

Mom Ant: Yes, thank you so much!

Dad Bee: You're welcome, my friends. We hope the Red Ants will let you through the farm soon.

Dad Ant: We hope so too.

Red Ant Mom: Look at this rotten corn. We can't eat it. It tastes horrible!

Red Ant Dad: There are still some good ones. We have to pick them out.

Red Ant Mom: Yes, but there are fewer good ones and more bad ones everyday.

Red Ant Dad: Well, we still have other kinds of food if we run out of corn.

Red Ant Mom: That's true.

Red Ant Dad: Oh no! Everything has gone rotten! Why?

Red Ant Mom: I don't know. It smells really bad everywhere. The water is dirty. We are almost out of food.

Red Ant Dad: What will we do? We don't know anything about farming.

Red Ant Mom: No, we don't.

Red Ant Dad: It looks like we will have to move again!

Dad Ant: Why do the red ants look so sad?

Mom Ant: And where are they going?

Red Ant Dad: Everything has gone rotten in the farm and we are out of food.

Red Ant Mom: We need to look for a new place to live.

Mom Ant: Oh no... How did that happen?

Red Ant Mom: Well, we don't know how to farm. When things go bad on us, we move.

Red Ant Dad: And that is why we can't share. We want to keep food for us as long as we can.

Dad and Mom Ants: Oh...I see!

Dad Ant: Hi Red Ants. We brought you some food. This basket should last you a few days.

Mom Ant: We were wondering if you would like to learn how to farm. We would love for you to stay and be part of our community. There is more than enough food and space for everyone.

Red Ant Dad: Wow...that would be wonderful! We would love to learn and stay here.

Red Ant Mom: Yes, we would. We are really embarrassed we did not share with you. We are sorry!

Dad Ant: It's ok. We understand.

Andrew Ant: Atom, I am glad you came by to play with me today.

Atom Ant: Me too. My Dad told me not to be afraid of the Red Ants. We have to live our lives.

Andrew Ant: My Dad said the same thing.

Annie Ant: Alex, can I play "catch" with you?

Arron Ant: Can I, too?

Alex Ant: Of course, guys! I am thrilled to see you outside again.

Andrew Ant: Arthur, the Red Ants look so sad. Do you want to ask them to play with us?

Arthur Ant: I don't know. I thought they didn't like us. You can ask them.

Andrew Ant: Hi, guys! Do you want to play with us? We will share our parachute.

Red Ant Brother: Are you sure? We were not nice to you all. The reason was because we were always teased about our fangs.

Andrew Ant: Oh no! I am sorry to hear that. We are not like that here. We welcome anyone and you can always play with us.

Red Ant Sister: Thank you! You are all very kind!

Andrew Ant: What a beautiful day, guys! And we have a new soccer member today. Welcome to the Red Ant!

Red Ant Brother: Thanks guys!

Annie Ant: You can be on our team. We are missing one player.

Red Ant Brother: Sure! Sounds good!

Alex Ant: It is always more fun to play together.

Red Ant Brother: Yes, I agree. It's much more fun to share!

Annie Ant: I am glad you think so. Yay! Let's play!

THE END

www.ingramcontent.com/pod-product-compliance
Lightning Source LLC
Chambersburg PA
CBHW041531280526
45792CB00004B/1455